THE
CRYSTAL
BOOK

THE
CRYSTAL
BOOK

Jennie Harding

First published in 2008 by
Ivy Press
The Old Candlemakers
West Street, Lewes
East Sussex, BN7 2NZ, UK
www.ivy-group.co.uk

British Library Cataloguing-in-Publication Data
A catalogue record for this book is available from
the British Library

ISBN-13: 978-1-905695-66-9
ISBN-10: 1-905695-66-7

Manufactured in China
10 9 8 7 6 5 4 3 2 1

Ivy Press
This book was conceived, designed,
and produced by iBall, an imprint of Ivy Press

Creative Director Peter Bridgewater
Publisher Jason Hook
Editorial Director Caroline Earle
Art Director Clare Harris
Senior Project Editor James Thomas
Designer Clare Barber
Photographer Andrew Perris

Contents

Healing the Body: Crystals and Chakras   45

Introduction

Welcome to *The Crystal Pack*, an exciting and fascinating introduction to the world of crystals and healing. This book and the seven colourful crystals that accompany it will set you off on a journey of discovery.

Crystals have fascinated human beings for thousands of years. From our earliest history, crystals have been used as jewellery, set into weapons and shields for protection, worn in crowns by kings and queens and carried as precious objects by ordinary people. Their shapes, colours, textures and light-reflective qualities make them especially attractive. As you explore these special stones with this book as a guide, you will begin to notice how different crystals appeal to you.

The world of crystals

All crystals are minerals, and most are formed inside the Earth itself. The ground you walk on may feel solid beneath your feet, but travel down a few miles into the Earth's crust and rock starts to liquefy until, at the core of the planet, it becomes a totally molten furnace. The heat of that furnace constantly pushes liquefied minerals up into fissures and spaces; a volcano exploding is literally forcing lava – molten rock – out onto the surface of the Earth. As minerals cool, they settle into layers where crystals begin to form. Sometimes larger pieces take shape inside

Smoky quartz

bubbles, gaps or cracks. The Earth beneath your feet is always changing; however, these processes are extremely slow and take millions of years. When you hold a crystal in your hand, you are touching something that has taken a long, long time to become that solid object.

Most crystals are inorganic, meaning that they come from elements that have never been alive. However, a few crystals are called organic minerals as they are originally from live sources. For example, amber is fossilised tree resin that has taken millions of years to harden; sometimes it even contains insects or pollen grains, perfectly preserved. Pearls are another example of an organic mineral, formed when sand irritates the lining inside certain oyster shells.

Amber

Crystals take different shapes according to the minerals they contain and the rate at which they cool during the formation process. Clear quartz, one of the most common of all crystals, tends to form geometric shapes, such as six-sided blades tapering to a point. Other types of quartz, known as agates, form in chunks and layers, like the carnelian in this pack. Crystals are found all over the world, and countries like the United States, Brazil, Myanmar and China are major sources. Today most stones are extracted through industrial mining.

When you first start collecting crystals it can be fascinating to learn about the many different types and their typical shapes, colours, textures and uses. Some are as smooth as glass, some have little indentations, others are rough or sharp. As you touch and hold your stones you will be able to feel the differences between them – and so you will begin to connect with them. This is the beginning of your personal journey.

Green Fluorite

What's in the Pack

Your pack contains seven Master Healing Crystals that you will learn to carry, care for, use and apply to your everyday life. These seven crystals have been specially selected to provide a wide range of tools for different purposes. Each crystal has different properties, which are summarised below. You will find more detailed individual profiles of these stones on pages 14–27.

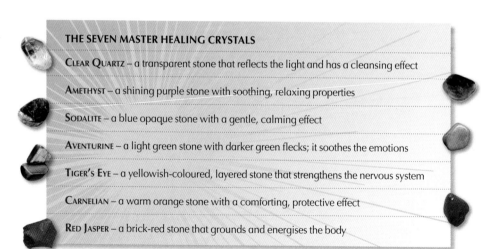

THE SEVEN MASTER HEALING CRYSTALS

CLEAR QUARTZ – a transparent stone that reflects the light and has a cleansing effect

AMETHYST – a shining purple stone with soothing, relaxing properties

SODALITE – a blue opaque stone with a gentle, calming effect

AVENTURINE – a light green stone with darker green flecks; it soothes the emotions

TIGER'S EYE – a yellowish-coloured, layered stone that strengthens the nervous system

CARNELIAN – a warm orange stone with a comforting, protective effect

RED JASPER – a brick-red stone that grounds and energises the body

The reason there are seven Master Healing Crystals is because there are seven major healing centres in the body, called chakras (*see pages 48–49*), which are important in crystal healing. Crystal healing is simply using crystals to help rebalance aspects of yourself that feel out of balance – perhaps your mind is too busy to relax, or you feel sad, or your body is tired and depleted. Specific crystals placed on your body in particular places can help to correct these imbalances, leaving you feeling refreshed and renewed. Using crystals regularly will also give you a sense of being supported by the healing powers of the Earth.

Observing your crystals

Place your stones on a clean white cloth. First, look at the variety of colours. Then look at the shapes of the stones and the way they catch the light. Clear quartz may reveal rainbow reflections, while the yellow tiger's eye shows layers that shimmer. Others, such as sodalite, are opaque and densely coloured. Get to know and sense your stones.

Cleansing Crystals

Your crystals are precious tools to help you improve your wellbeing, so it is important to look after them. They look beautiful displayed in a special place, or, if you prefer, you can store them in a cloth bag or a box.

Cleansing your crystals

Before you use your set of stones for healing, they need to be cleansed and tuned to your energy frequency for maximum effect. Simply pour some pure spring water into a clear glass bowl. Place your stones in the water and leave them overnight, then drain the water and dry them with a clean, soft cloth. Pick up each stone in turn, close your eyes and say aloud, 'May this crystal work for my highest good and the good of others.' This will programme your stones for use.

Repeat this water cleansing method each time you use your stones in a crystal healing treatment.

YOUR SEVEN MASTER HEALING CRYSTALS

Master Crystals

We shall now explore the crystals in your pack in more depth, finding out about each stone individually – its features, uses in history and healing effects. We will then look at simple ways to place stones on the body for a healing effect. First, however, let us consider the true meaning of Master Healing Crystals.

Crystals through history

Since ancient times, specific crystals have been considered to have particular powers. The Old Testament book of Exodus, for example, contains a long description of the making of a special breastplate, a heavy ceremonial ornament to be worn by a high priest who would act as an intermediary between the people and God. Into this breastplate would be set specific stones – topaz, emerald, sapphire, diamond, agate, amethyst, beryl, onyx and jasper are easily recognisable examples listed in the biblical account. These stones, set in gold, were considered essential in making the breastplate a powerful object to amplify the energy of the high priest.

The ancient Egyptians also frequently used crystals in gold collars, necklaces, head ornaments and crowns for their nobility and kings. Stones such as sodalite and lapis lazuli, both bright blue in colour, were inlaid in gold alongside contrasting

Quartz point

agates such as red jasper and black onyx. The stones were not only selected for their colour but also for their sacred meanings – for example, the blue colour of lapis lazuli was associated with the heavens, while the specks of golden pyrite it contains were linked to the sun god, Ra.

The Aztecs and Incas of Mexico and South America revered green stones like jade and emerald because their gods inhabited the lush green jungles that were their natural environment. Green stones were considered sacred to those gods and adorned the Aztec and Inca rulers, who served as the living representatives of the gods on Earth.

Already you can see that some of your seven Master Healing Crystals have been featured in these accounts – agate (the agates in your pack are carnelian, tiger's eye and aventurine), amethyst, jasper and sodalite. These link you to the sacred traditions of past civilisations. The final stone in your pack is clear quartz, which has been used as a healing tool for thousands of years. Today, professional crystal healers often use clear quartz wands – that is, naturally tapering points of quartz – to direct and clear the main energy channels of the body.

Crystals and colour

The crystals in your pack are also considered master healers because they represent the seven colours of the rainbow. Healing practitioners of many different disciplines use the seven colours – or seven rays, as they are sometimes called – to bring different frequencies or types of energy into the body. Red, orange, and yellow frequencies are warm and energising; green, the colour of plants, promotes growth; and blue, violet and white are cool and cleansing.

Quartz point

Clear Quartz

Clear quartz – or rock quartz as it is sometimes called – is what many people visualise when they think of the word crystal. A classic stone in any collection, quartz is a common mineral also known as silicon dioxide. It is found all over the world and particularly beautiful examples come from Brazil. Quartz occurs in a wide variety of shapes, sizes and forms. In its raw state it forms points called terminations with six geometric facets; when polished, these pieces often display lovely rainbow reflections.

Physical effects

Clear quartz is used in healing to cleanse the energetic field around the human body and free it from any negativity. This cleansing creates the potential for a harmonious realignment of mind, body and spirit, enhancing physical and mental wellbeing. This crystal also retains the energy imprint of the person receiving healing, so it is important to purify quartz by soaking it in water after healing sessions, before reuse. Clear quartz also stimulates the immune system and strengthens the nervous system; for example, when worn as a pendant, it can help to protect the wearer from pollution and negative energy in the environment.

Quartz tumblestone

Spiritual uses

In crystal healing, clear quartz is used to amplify and expand the mind into higher levels of spiritual consciousness. Meditating with a piece of clear quartz can be inspiring, and often results in flashes of intuition or awareness beyond the level of everyday life, which in turn can help to solve problems or personal issues.

Keeping a small piece of clear quartz near your bed can help you remember your dreams, while larger pieces of quartz placed around the home or in the office can help cleanse negativity from the environment, as well as promote clear thinking and improved concentration.

Professional crystal healers use specific varieties of clear quartz to rebalance the body's energy flow, for example, 'self healed' pieces of quartz that have broken during formation and then sealed themselves may be particularly effective.

Clear quartz (raw)

Amethyst

Amethyst is a type of quartz coloured by iron or aluminium and is one of the most powerful and beautiful of all crystals. It is typically a vivid purple in colour, varying from pale lavender shades to deep violet. Amethyst occurs in various natural shapes such as clusters of small points, large points with geometric faces or huge enclosed masses called *vugs* in which amethyst crystals grow towards the centre of what was once a large bubble in lava. Smaller pieces of amethyst are often smoothed and polished to bring out their colour. Brazil and Mexico are sources of high-quality amethyst.

Physical effects

On a physical level, amethyst helps to soothe headaches, migraines and feelings of mental overload, especially when placed just above the nose between the eyebrows during a healing treatment. It also can be placed on

Amethyst tumblestone

computers or taped over mobile phones to protect sensitive individuals from electromagnetic stress. Placing a piece of amethyst near the bed or under the pillow at night improves sleep quality and provides a refreshing rest, free from troubling dreams. Carrying or wearing amethyst calms the nervous system, which is easily depleted by the stresses and strains of everyday life. Amethyst helps you maintain a sense of inner peace.

Amethyst (raw)

Spiritual uses

Revered as a healing tool since ancient times, amethyst is regarded as a Master Healing Crystal for enhancing spiritual expansion and is often worn at the brow to stimulate the third-eye chakra (*see pages 64–65*). It is also featured in the design of many royal crowns and diadems as a symbol of spiritual power. Amethyst's vivid purple colour soothes and clears the mind, enhancing psychic perceptions and increasing sensitivity to healing energy. Applied to the brow during a healing session, amethyst helps to free the mind from everyday burdens and opens perception of new levels of self-awareness. This awareness can lead to a new understanding of one's unique purpose and generate the inspiration to make positive changes in life.

Sodalite

Sodalite is so named because it is high in the mineral sodium. It also contains aluminium. It is typically a vivid blue colour, crossed with white veins and specks of paler blue. These veins, or lines, in its structure show that it forms in horizontal layers. It is classified as *igneous*, which means it is formed by molten lava that squeezes its way into geologic cavities. Sodalite is often found in deposits close to active volcanoes, such as Vesuvius in southern Italy. The ancient Egyptians used sodalite along with bright blue lapis lazuli to create a stunning colour contrast in their gold jewellery, as well as to symbolise the heavens. Polished sodalite has a smooth, silky feel and is also quite light in weight.

Physical effects

Sodalite tumblestone

Sodalite supports the throat, voice and vocal chords and is a useful stone to wear or carry if you are a teacher, singer or a regular public speaker. It also protects the throat from infection and supports the immune system. Sodalite is a good stone to place under the pillow to speed recovery from illnesses such as colds or influenza. Its vivid blue colour and cooling energy frequency can balance and regulate blood pressure as well as cool fever.

Sodalite (raw)

Spiritual uses

Sodalite can clear the mind when feelings of anger, conflict, resentment or frustration get in the way of clear thinking. This stone supports mental clarity, peace and clear decision making, aiding communication both in one-to-one situations and in groups. Placed over the throat, sodalite encourages clear communication unclouded by negativity. It connects the mind with the soul, the spiritual aspect of oneself, and enhances intuition. Meditate with sodalite to find new angles and new solutions to problems or situations that seem to repeat themselves. Sodalite also expands your awareness of personal truth, goals and life purpose and helps you express these things to others.

Aventurine

This soft green-coloured crystal is a special type of quartz known as *microcrystalline*. Its structure resembles tiny sugar granules packed closely together. Aventurine also contains specks of a mineral called *fuchsite* that create a sparkling, slightly darker green sheen within the stone itself. India is one of the most common sources of aventurine, which is used to carve statues, boxes and jewellery. It can occur in massive deposits from which large slabs can be cut; thus, it is a popular ornamental stone used as an inlay with marble in floors, or even in the carving of pillars.

Physical effects

Aventurine soothes the heart and promotes healthy circulation, giving a sense of physical and emotional vitality to the whole body. It encourages cell renewal, especially after accidents or physical trauma. It also helps regenerate physical energy, creating the impetus for growth and the strength to make new beginnings in life. Aventurine is a lovely gentle stone to use with children. To remedy sleeplessness or aid in recovery from childhood illnesses, place a small stone under the pillow or try putting a piece in the child's bath (*see pages 40–41*). Large pieces placed in the home or office transmit a sense of tranquility.

Aventurine tumblestone

Spiritual uses

Aventurine is linked to the area in the middle of the chest known as the heart chakra (*see pages 60–61*). This area is positively influenced by emotions such as love, but can also be depleted by feelings of isolation or sadness. Placing or wearing aventurine over the heart area soothes negative feelings and brings out the warmth of love and a sensation of being nurtured. It also promotes the releasing of the past, allowing the wearer to look forward with hope. The green colour of aventurine reminds us of nature and the constant cycles of change, rebirth and renewal in the plant kingdom.

Aventurine (raw)

Tiger's Eye

This beautiful stone contains bands of gold and brown; if you turn it back and forth in the light, you will see a special kind of shimmer effect. Tiger's eye is a kind of quartz, but it has formed in an unusual way. Bands of a reflective mineral called *crocidolite* interweave with the silicon dioxide structure of the quartz, creating a 'cat's-eye' effect as light rays bounce back and forth in the stone. This fascinating quality has made tiger's eye a popular stone for thousands of years, and pieces of ancient jewellery with tiger's eye set in gold have been found in the Middle East and Egypt. Good-quality stones come from the U.S. and South Africa.

Physical effects

This crystal is like an energy battery for the system, helping to build physical vitality and strength, improving mental focus and providing stamina. Traditionally, tiger's eye was believed to aid the functioning of the eyes, while also stimulating 'clear vision' in life. Tiger's eye maintains the circulation and energises the nervous system. It also calms stress and tension in the abdomen, easing feelings of fear or butterflies in the stomach, making it a good stone to carry during exams, visits to the dentist or under any other circumstances in which you feel challenged!

Tiger's eye tumblestone

Tiger's eye (raw)

Spiritual uses

The alternating colour bands in tiger's eye symbolise the grounding of solar energy (gold) into the Earth (brown). This stone helps integrate spiritual inspiration into the practical side of everyday life. The Buddhists have a saying for this – 'Before enlightenment, chop wood, carry water; after enlightenment, chop wood, carry water.' This means that there needs to be a balance between the mental and the physical; between ideas and action. Meditating with tiger's eye can turn creative inspiration into a realistic plan for moving forwards or taking a new direction in life.

Carnelian

This stone is one of many types of microcrystalline quartz made of tiny granules of silicon dioxide. Carnelian gets its colour from iron impurities that turn it orange. It can vary in colour from apricot to deep orange-red, and some stones contain paler bands. India, Uruguay and Brazil are good sources of this stone. Carnelian forms in huge masses or blocks, and is often carved and polished into large spheres to show off the intensity of its colour. It has been carved into beads, rings and other types of jewellery since ancient times. The Egyptians often used it on gold collars, as a contrasting stone to black onyx and blue lapis lazuli.

Physical effects

Carnelian is often seen as a comforting stone – a useful crystal to wear or carry to provide warm and nurturing energy. It soothes physical stress symptoms such as tightness in the chest or shortness of breath, and calms feelings of anger, anxiety or fear. Carnelian speeds healing after physical trauma, accident or injury to the body; keep a piece under your pillow or place it in your bath (*see pages 40–41*). It warms the circulation, builds vitality and is an excellent stone for stimulating sexual energy.

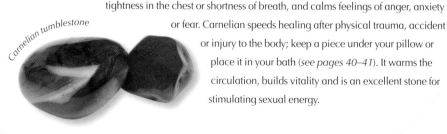

Carnelian tumblestone

Carnelian (raw)

Spiritual uses

In medieval times, carnelian was often carried as an amulet or worn as a ring because it was believed to be a good source of protection against negative influences. In crystal healing today, carnelian is used to promote courage in the face of challenges, as well as to strengthen the heart, enabling the individual to make sound choices. It soothes emotional tension and stress and brings peace and warmth to body and mind. It also helps dissolve old feelings of anger and resentment, replacing them with understanding and compassion. Wear it or meditate with it to encourage openness towards others.

Red Jasper

Jasper is another type of microcrystalline quartz, densely coloured and opaque. Red jasper is coloured by iron oxide, giving it an intense brick-red shade; jasper can also be yellow, green, blue, purple and brown. It is one of the most common types of crystal available to collectors; fine examples come from Brazil and India. Red jasper has been a popular stone for hundreds of years. The Romans were fond of it, often carving it into cameos – delicate portraits of gods, goddesses or people – and signet rings, which boasted a crest that was pressed into wax to seal letters or important documents to identify the sender.

Physical effects

Red jasper deeply energises the body, aiding in recovery from physical exhaustion, low energy levels and lack of vitality. It is an excellent stone to use in the bath to help regeneration after illness (*see pages 40–41*). It warms the

Red jasper tumblestone

circulation and increases physical strength. Red jasper also has a strong protective effect on the aura – the energy field around the human body – which can be depleted by environmental factors including noise, pollution and electromagnetic waves. Carrying or wearing red jasper provides a protective shield against these negative influences.

Spiritual uses

Red jasper is a wonderful stone to use while meditating if you are at the beginning of a new project. It helps to generate the physical energy you need to bring your ideas to life. It promotes enjoyment of new experiences, zest for life and enthusiasm to carry you forward. During healing sessions (*see pages 32–37*), red jasper is often placed between the feet to anchor the body because it has a strong grounding effect. If you ever feel unsteady or slightly 'out of your body', holding red jasper will always bring you back to earth so you feel centred again.

Red jasper (raw)

Working with Layouts

Having explored all seven Master Healing Crystals, now we will look at how to use them. Crystal healing uses a method called a 'layout', which is simply a way of arranging crystals on or around the body. The layout creates an energy field in which a person simply lies at rest for about fifteen minutes or so – it is like taking an 'energy bath', after which both body and mind feel restored.

Setting up a layout

Crystal healing requires some preparation. Make sure your space is clean and tidy. Lighting a candle creates a peaceful atmosphere. Place a soft blanket or rug on the floor, with a pillow on top of it, and let your friend lie down comfortably on their back. Put a shawl or blanket over them to keep them warm. Next, select the crystals you need for the layout and place them in position. You might want to play some gentle music while your friend relaxes and you sit quietly nearby. It is important to not speak during the session; this is a subtle form of healing and resting peacefully in the crystal energy is all that is needed.

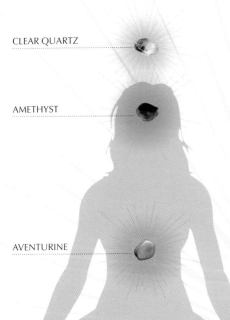

CLEAR QUARTZ

AMETHYST

AVENTURINE

A simple first layout

This combination requires clear quartz, amethyst and aventurine – three stones to balance the mind and emotions. This layout will help someone who is feeling emotionally stressed or who has a conflict between head and heart. Place the clear quartz on the floor above the middle of the head, the amethyst gently on the centre of the forehead and the aventurine over the centre of the chest above the breastbone. After about fifteen minutes, remove the stones, offer your friend some water to drink and discuss any feelings that arose during the session.

Simple Crystal Layouts

On pages 32–37 you will find three different layouts, called Grounding, Building and Expansive. These are examples of the different effects of crystal healing layouts. As energy is constantly changing from one state to another, we need different kinds of help according to the way we feel inside.

Grounding layout

This is a stabilising pattern that can bring a person back 'into the body'. It suits people who feel physically depleted and in need of regeneration. Grounding also helps to centre people who are feeling scatterbrained or unfocused.

Building layout

This pattern works on the core energy of the system centred around the solar plexus, just under the curve of the ribcage. It creates a sense of purpose and strength and helps people who are emotionally stressed and tense.

Expansive layout

This layout encourages spiritual awareness and psychic perception. It helps people who are stuck in repetitive mental patterns or stress. Most people need to experience the grounding or building layouts first before this one is attempted, in order to create a stable energy platform for the powerful energy of expansion.

Practised in turn, these three layouts create a six-pointed energy star – an ancient symbol of a human being with body, mind and spirit in harmony. Choosing the right layout is important – it depends how your friend is feeling. Discuss this between you before deciding which layout is most suitable.

Crystal layouts are always practised between two people – one giving, the other receiving. This ensures that support and feedback can be shared regarding the session – this sharing can be quite powerful. If you want to work with crystals alone, it is best to meditate with one stone at a time.

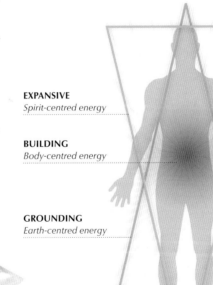

EXPANSIVE
Spirit-centred energy

BUILDING
Body-centred energy

GROUNDING
Earth-centred energy

Grounding Layout

When was the last time you walked barefoot? Perhaps it was in the summertime, when you walked on a green lawn and felt the grass beneath your feet, or maybe on a holiday when you placed your feet in warm sand, feeling its texture between your toes. These sensations carry a positive memory because they are precious moments when your feet made full contact with the Earth. This is 'grounding' – a sense of deep connection with the planet on which we live. Grounding helps people who 'live in their heads' or who feel pulled in all directions with no sense of focus.

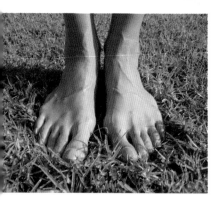

Connecting with the Earth

As well as walking barefoot, lying on the ground is another way to make contact with the Earth, to establish this sense of connection with the surrounding environment. Crystals arranged around the body in a grounding layout add extra energy to help restore and re-energise the physical body. This layout is an especially useful one to try if you are feeling tired and depleted.

Setting up the layout

Prepare a healing space as directed on pages 28–29. Next place your clear quartz on the floor near the top of your friend's head, your carnelian on the lower abdomen and your red jasper between the feet. Allow a resting period of 10–15 minutes, then share some water and discuss any feelings the layout brought up.

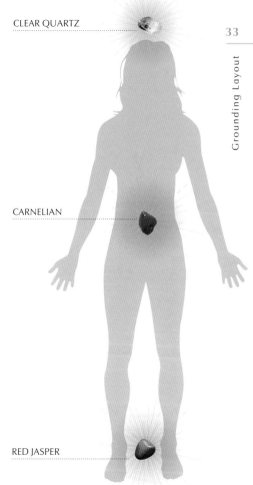

CARNELIAN

RED JASPER

Building Layout

Imagine a diver on a high board, about to take the plunge. Before he even leaves the surface of the board, there is a moment where all his muscles draw in and prepare for the sudden spring that will take him into the movement of the dive. That moment of drawing in, of gathering energy into the core of the body and all the muscles, is an example of 'building' energy. It's the moment before expansion, before the leap. It is also the pause before every breath you take.

Fuelling growth

Building energy is centred in the solar plexus, a vital area in the middle of the trunk just below the ribcage. This area is depleted by mental stress, aggression and being on constant alert. Crystals help to restore and revitalise this area with plenty of energy to fuel new growth in life. This layout also replenishes the nervous system after periods of intense stress.

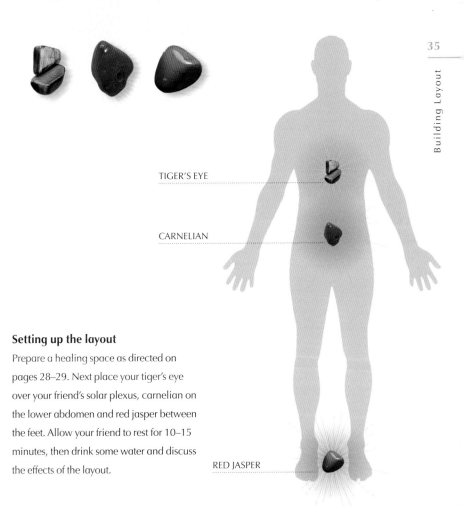

TIGER'S EYE

CARNELIAN

RED JASPER

Setting up the layout

Prepare a healing space as directed on
pages 28–29. Next place your tiger's eye
over your friend's solar plexus, carnelian on
the lower abdomen and red jasper between
the feet. Allow your friend to rest for 10–15
minutes, then drink some water and discuss
the effects of the layout.

Expansive Layout

Next time there is a full moon, go outside and look at it floating in the night sky among the stars. There is too much above you to see it all in one glance; you have to turn your head to take it all in. As you stand there, become aware of the vastness of space, of stars so far away their light has taken years to reach you. Let your mind relax. You may find a deep peace enveloping you, a sense of the vastness, even though you can't see it all. That feeling of space beyond yourself to which you can connect is 'expansive' energy.

Reaching beyond

Expansive energy helps you to experience what 'spirit' really means to you, and to connect spiritually with your surrounding environment. Crystals arranged around the head, forehead and throat serve to enhance this higher frequency. It is very important to be grounded and centred first before working at this higher level, in order to feel balanced and secure. Make sure to try the grounding and building layouts before attempting this one.

Setting up the layout

Prepare a healing space as directed on pages 28–29. Place your clear quartz on the ground above the top of your friend's head, your amethyst between the eyebrows, sodalite on the throat and red jasper between the feet. Allow your friend to rest for 10–15 minutes, then drink some water together and talk about the effects of the layout.

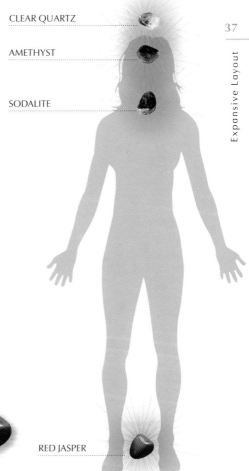

CLEAR QUARTZ

AMETHYST

SODALITE

RED JASPER

Making Crystal Waters and Elixirs

A simple way to experience the healing effects of crystals is to soak them in water and then drink the water. Water is a unique substance, capable of absorbing and holding the energetic properties of a stone, and these are taken into the body as the water is consumed. In medieval times, soaking crystals in water or wine and then drinking the liquid was considered very beneficial to one's health. Some of the most effective crystals to use in this way are listed below.

Crystal waters

Take a clean glass pitcher and fill it with pure spring water. Place a cleansed crystal inside the pitcher and leave it on a windowsill where it will receive strong light, preferably sunlight if possible. The light facilitates the transfer of crystal energies into the water. Leave the pitcher for at least an hour before drinking the water. You can refill it as the water level goes down, but remember to let it stand for a while to energise again. Drink crystal water on the day it is made. Good crystals to choose are clear quartz for a detoxifying and refreshing effect; pink rose quartz, which is soothing and relaxing to body and mind; and sodalite, to cool and calm the emotions. Choose any crystal that appeals to you in a given moment – trust your instinct.

Crystal elixirs

The following method is used to make crystal remedies called *elixirs*, which have a shelf life of at least two years. Take a small glass bowl and fill it with spring water. Place a cleansed crystal of your choice in the water. Let the bowl stand in strong sunlight for at least an hour. Carefully pour some of the energised water into a large, dark-glass bottle, until half-full, then add the same amount of brandy. Shake the two together and place in a dark cupboard for up to a week, shaking occasionally. This process makes the elixir, which you take by adding half a teaspoonful to a glass of water and sipping it slowly.

Suitable crystals for elixirs include amethyst to promote mental clarity and calm, red jasper for physical energy, aventurine for relaxation and peace and clear quartz for creativity and inspiration. If you prefer, you can combine different crystals – for example, clear quartz and amethyst together for clarity and relaxation – if you would like more than one property in the remedy.

> **WARNING**
>
> *All the stones in this pack are safe to use to make waters or elixirs. However, if you want to use other stones, make sure they do not contain arsenic, lead or mercury because these substances are extremely toxic. Ask a professional crystal healer for advice if you are unsure.*

Crystals in the Bath

Swimming in the sea, where the combination of water, sunlight and crystals creates an incredible environment, you are literally bathed in crystal energy. When you get out of the ocean water, you feel refreshed and re-energised because of the light, water and crystals working together.

Crystal baths

It is possible to re-create some of the ocean's effects at home by placing crystals in your bath. The water will absorb their properties and increase your relaxation. This treatment can be further enhanced by adding some rock or Dead Sea mineral salts to the bath – a cupful is enough. The salt also deeply cleanses your skin. Choose one crystal or a combination of your favourite stones – you can select them for their properties, or let your instinct choose colours that suit your mood. Simply place the stones in the water when you take your bath and relax in the healing water for at least 30 minutes. Smooth polished stones are best – don't use sharp points, as they may be uncomfortable!

Here is a reminder of your Master Healing Stones and how you might like to use them in the bath:

MASTER HEALING STONES AND THEIR PROPERTIES
CLEAR QUARTZ – refreshing and cleansing to mind and body
AMETHYST – soothing and calming, good for promoting sound sleep
SODALITE – relaxing, for a peaceful inner feeling
AVENTURINE – calming and nurturing to the emotions
TIGER'S EYE – strengthening and energising to mind and body
CARNELIAN – warming and enveloping, for deep relaxation
RED JASPER – energising to the physical body

Another excellent crystal to use in the bath is pink rose quartz: it is incredibly gentle and soothing, a wonderful aid to inner peace and relaxation, and works for both children and adults to calm overactive emotions like anger or irritability.

Crystal baths are best taken in the evening, especially if you are using stones to relax you and improve your sleep. Try adding one or two drops of lavender essential oil to the water to bring an extra relaxing element to the bath. Essential oils from plants work well with crystal energies, because plants grow in soil, which is full of minerals.

Crystals around the Home

Crystals are beautiful and once you start to collect them you will want to look at them all the time. Their colours stand out in any environment and they can be used in many creative ways to add energetic qualities to any space. Using your intuition is the best way to decide where to place crystals, but the following suggestions may inspire you.

Altars and sacred spaces

In some countries, such as Japan and India, many houses have a special space or altar where fresh flowers, candles and sacred objects are placed and refreshed on a daily basis. This practice creates a clear and peaceful energy inside a home and honours the spiritual beliefs of those who live there. Setting up an altar or a sacred space is easy – cover a table with a beautiful cloth, then add flowers in a vase and a candle in a holder. Lighting the candle and burning some incense to perfume the air is a lovely prelude to meditation. Place crystals on the altar to add their energy and colour to the display.

Crystals in the garden

Crystals come from the Earth and are therefore welcome outside in a garden space, especially as part of a water feature, for example, where they will sparkle in the sunlight and their colour can be vividly reflected. Smaller stones can be set in mosaics or made into mobiles to hang in bushes or trees where their facets and polished surfaces will catch the sunlight.

Placing large crystals

In addition to small tumblestones or points, crystals are also available as large raw pieces, polished spheres or carved flame shapes, which can add a strong presence to your home, office or outdoor space. When you buy a large piece of crystal, soak it in water for at least two days to cleanse it thoroughly of any residual energies it may carry from previous handling, then dry it with a soft, clean cloth before bringing it into the desired space. Think carefully about where to place it. Bedrooms are not ideal because of the high level of energy emitted by a large piece of crystal. Living rooms, conservatories or office spaces are better choices. Remember that stones have different qualities – rose quartz has a gentle presence, whereas smoky quartz is a powerful environmental cleanser, and clear quartz is like a power battery. Take time to get to know and feel a large stone and sense where it needs to be.

Clear quartz (raw)

Wearing Crystals

Crystals have been worn as jewellery for thousands of years. In ancient times, crystals and precious stones were chosen to adorn different parts of the body according to their special meanings. Diamonds, rubies and sapphires were used in ancient India to decorate crowns and headpieces for kings and princes – these stones were considered sacred, adding their energy to the person wearing them.

Choosing and using crystal jewellery

When you choose crystals to wear, think about their meaning. So, if your emotions need calming, try aventurine in a pendant over your heart. By thinking like this you will benefit from crystals' energies as you wear them.

Crystals absorb negativity, so cleanse your crystal jewellery, especially if you wear it often, by soaking in spring water, preferably overnight. If someone gives you a piece of jewellery, cleanse it before you wear it, so it can be reprogrammed to your own energy frequency. Precious stones like opals or emeralds should not be soaked as this makes them brittle. Soaking works for hard crystals like quartz or gems like ruby, diamond or sapphire.

HEALING THE BODY:
CRYSTALS AND CHAKRAS

Healing the Body

In this chapter we will explore the energy system of the chakras, to show how crystals can be even more effective as healing tools when aligned with specific chakra energies. The word 'heal' comes from the old German word *hael* meaning 'whole' or 'holy'. This double meaning implies that to be healed means to be restored to a state of wholeness, as well as to be put in touch with something sacred. So what does that mean, exactly?

Seeking wholeness

Wholeness is something that cannot be forced, measured or calculated. It is a feeling, a sense of being part of something that is supportive and greater than you. Traditional Native American beliefs hold that everything is alive – not only people, animals, birds, fish, plants and trees – but also rocks, rivers, streams, lakes and the sea. From this viewpoint, all life, and everything that surrounds us, is sacred. In the past, young people went on special quests into nature as part of the ritual of becoming adults, communicating with the natural world and learning to become part of it. Being part of nature or something bigger than the self is the meaning of wholeness. When you feel a sense of wholeness, it is like relaxing into the arms of someone who comforts you. Your stress melts away and you are at peace. Working with crystals, the gifts of the Earth, brings their energies and qualities into contact with you. These energies help you reconnect to a deeper sense of yourself.

A sense of the sacred

The quality of being sacred is not linked to a particular religion. All the world's major faiths have their ways of expressing what it means. Sacredness is found in a reverence for life; a gentle and loving sense of peace. A sacred state of being can be reached through prayer, meditation or receiving healing treatment. In a state of reverence, a feeling of deep contentment and calm can permeate the mind and body, and stresses or anxieties disappear.

Thousands of years ago, civilisations in China and India developed healing systems that survive today, systems based on the idea that the body is more than a physical entity but it also has an energy system that powers it – similar to the electrical current in a battery. When the energy level is lowered or the supply is cut, the bodily system cannot function and an adjustment is needed to restore balance. The energy itself is a link to the source of all life. Some Native Americans call this energy 'the Great Spirit'; some people call it God, or the Creator. Healing brings that special energy back into the body, and enables it to be renewed. Crystals can hold and direct or channel healing energy.

What are the Chakras?

The word *chakra* comes from the ancient Indian Sanskrit language, and it means 'wheel'. In this ancient healing system, seven major chakras or wheels are positioned along the column of the spine. In crystal healing, by aligning crystals with chakra energies in healing layouts, you can increase their effectiveness as healing tools.

Energy currents

People with extra sensory perception or psychic abilities are able to 'see' energy as an aura surrounding the human body. Such individuals have reported that the chakras can be seen to open and close. Moreover, they have also observed the chakras spinning in a spiral motion, somewhat like water in a whirlpool. When all the chakras are open and are functioning properly, the human body will receive cosmic or divine energy like a current flowing through it in all the correct frequencies.

CROWN – *Located in the centre of the top of the head, this chakra is linked to spiritual consciousness.*

THIRD EYE – *Located in the middle of the brow between the eyebrows, this chakra is related to intuition and leaps of awareness.*

THROAT – *Located in the hollow of the throat, this chakra corresponds to communication.*

HEART – *Located in the centre of the chest over the breastbone, this chakra is linked to love and compassion.*

SOLAR PLEXUS – *Found just under the breastbone, where the ribs curve upward, this chakra relates to mental awareness and strong instincts.*

SACRAL – *Located three finger-widths below the navel, this chakra corresponds to relationships and sexual energy*

ROOT – *Located at the base of the spine (coccyx), this chakra is connected to physical survival and power.*

How the Chakras Work

The ancient Indian healing system of Ayurveda teaches that the seven major chakras are energy centres that work at different levels or frequencies. These are vital, because cosmic or divine energy is so powerful that if it were not lowered in frequency, the human body would not be able to contain or use it. The chakras allow cosmic energy to enter the body to provide fuel for all levels of human activity.

Chakras and hormones

Ayurvedic tradition also teaches that the seven major chakra centres are linked to the body's main hormone centres. Hormones are chemical messengers the brain sends to different areas of the body to achieve specific effects. Hormone centres serve as the interface between the chakra energy system and the physical body.

The crown chakra is linked to the pineal gland, which controls our response to light and dark and helps us fall asleep. The third eye chakra is associated with the pituitary gland, the master hormone centre. The throat chakra corresponds to the thyroid, which governs metabolism and cellular repair. The heart chakra is connected with the thymus gland, a centre for the immune system. The solar plexus chakra relates to the pancreas gland and the hormone insulin. The sacral chakra is linked to the sex glands and their hormones, while the root chakra links to the adrenal glands and adrenaline.

CROWN	These energies feel cool and are of a high frequency. They are linked to spiritual opening and enhanced self-awareness.
THIRD EYE	
THROAT	
HEART	This is the bridge between the physical and spiritual chakras, and is the place of love and growth, a middle frequency of gentle warmth.
SOLAR PLEXUS	These energies are linked to physical processes in the body; needed for activity, reproduction, and survival, they feel hot and are at a low frequency.
SACRAL	
ROOT	

Chakras, colours and frequencies

Ayurvedic tradition assigns colours to the chakras to illustrate their effects. In the West, since the 19th century, the seven colours of the rainbow have been used to depict the seven chakra levels and are used by Western professional spiritual healers to this day. This is an adaptation that has developed during the re-emergence of spiritual healing practice in the 20th and 21st centuries and it differs from traditional Ayurvedic representation.

The frequencies of the chakras correspond to light vibrations, not temperature: red, orange and yellow light frequencies vibrate slowly, while blue and purple rays are faster. Spiritual healers sense the lower vibrations as heat and the higher ones as cool when they place their hands on a person's body.

Full Crystal and Chakra Layout

This special layout incorporates all seven of the Master Healing Crystals. It is a complete crystal and chakra healing treatment, which will regulate and refresh all levels of energy. If performed regularly (for example, on a weekly basis), this beautiful layout can help ease stress levels as well as enhance feelings of being centred and at peace.

Preparation

It is best to perform this layout when the recipient has time to rest afterwards. This will help the body to adjust to energetic changes brought about by the healing activity of the crystals.

Make sure you have cleansed your crystals in pure spring water before each treatment. Prepare the healing space carefully by cleaning and dusting the room and bringing in some fresh flowers in a vase. Light a candle and some incense if you wish. Gentle music playing in the background also creates a pleasant atmosphere and helps to enhance the relaxation process. Spread a clean white sheet and pillow on the ground, and ask your friend to lie down on their back. Drape them with a soft blanket for extra warmth, then ask your friend to take some calm, slow breaths.

The treatment

Say quietly, 'May the combined energies of these crystals balance your system and bring you peace.' Sit quietly with your friend for about 15 minutes. Should sleep ensue, gently place a hand on your friend's shoulder to slowly awaken them. Before your friend sits up, encourage deep breathing and a focus of attention on the body, noticing any areas of warmth or coolness. These are signs of the crystal and chakra energies working. Remove the crystals from the body and place them in a bowl of spring water to cleanse them. Offer a drink of water to flush any physical or energetic toxins out of the system. Sit quietly for a while longer, to fully absorb the energy of the treatment.

Some people see colours or images, or feel sensations, while receiving healing. Others just feel a general sense of relaxation. All people respond in the way that is right for them, so trust in the process.

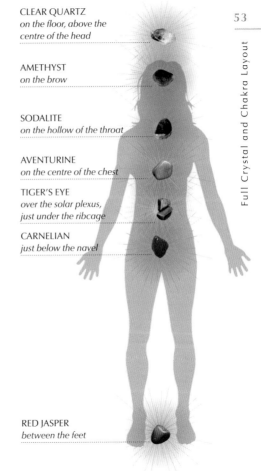

CLEAR QUARTZ
on the floor, above the centre of the head

AMETHYST
on the brow

SODALITE
on the hollow of the throat

AVENTURINE
on the centre of the chest

TIGER'S EYE
over the solar plexus, just under the ribcage

CARNELIAN
just below the navel

RED JASPER
between the feet

Root Chakra

The root chakra is located at the base of the spine in the coccyx, or tail bone. This important chakra maintains and enhances the life force that we need to live and function each day. Root chakra energy is also connected to the physical body and its strength. The ancient Indian name for this chakra is *muladhara*, which means 'root' or 'central support'. Imagine a tall tree – it cannot stay upright without strong roots to support it.

Main functions

The root chakra connects us to the physical energy in the body, which corresponds to our survival in the world. Without this energy, we would not have the strength for physical tasks that ensure our nourishment and security. Strong root chakra energy gives a feeling of being safe and grounded; that is, feeling the support of the Earth on which we walk. The root chakra also corresponds to our blood, the physical manifestation of the human life force which, of course, is bright red – the colour of root chakra energy.

Root chakra issues

The root chakra is linked to the adrenal glands, which are actively involved in maintaining the physical energy of the body. The adrenals can easily become depleted by high levels of physical or emotional stress, resulting in lower back pain or feelings of a lack of support. An overburdened root chakra needs plenty of physical rest, good food and sleep to help replenish its energy.

How crystals can help

With its strong reddish-orange colour and its grounding properties, red jasper is an excellent stone to boost root chakra energy. In healing layouts, red jasper can either be placed over the lower abdomen or between the feet, since root chakra energy extends from the lower back all the way down the legs. Another good root chakra-enhancing stone is ruby, which increases the life force in the body and enhances the circulation.

Red jasper

Sacral Chakra

The sacral chakra is located at the level of the sacrum, a triangular fused bone that is centred between the hips. On the front of the body, this chakra is found by measuring three finger-widths below the navel. Its Sanskrit name is *svadhisthana*, meaning 'dwelling place'. This chakra is considered to be the focal point for human creative energy, the sacred force known as sexuality that creates new life, and the drive to bring ideas into physical manifestation. The colour of this chakra is a warm orange shade, which has positive effects on the emotions.

Main functions

The sacral chakra relates to reproductive function; it balances and maintains the energy of the lower back, hips and sexual organs. Strong sacral chakra energy is visible in a belly dancer, for example – the circular and spiral movements of the hips keep this area open and mobile. Belly dancing was

Carnelian

originally developed to help women stay supple in preparation for childbirth. Sacral chakra energy is also important in men, because it maintains the health of the prostate gland, vital for healthy sexual function.

Sacral chakra issues

Premenstrual fatigue, lower back pain or painful menstruation may be due
to a woman's depleted sacral chakra energy. Any issues involving sexual
disinterest or problems with intimacy suggest a need for replenishment
of sacral chakra energy and may also require professional counselling.
Dancing, t'ai chi and yoga all work well as re-energising activities.
Moreover, the aromas of essential oils such as sandalwood or jasmine
can also help to stimulate the sacral chakra.

How crystals can help

Carnelian works well with the sacral chakra, because it is an energising
stone with a lovely replenishing effect. Place it in the bath to raise low sacral
chakra energy, or use it to make a crystal water to drink throughout the day.
Another sacral energiser is amber (in particular,
the darker orange-coloured pieces),
which energises the sacral chakra
and helps to uplift the emotions.

Solar Plexus Chakra

Named *manipura* ('lustrous jewel') in Sanskrit, the solar plexus chakra is located just below the middle of the ribcage at the base of the breastbone. The colour of this chakra is brilliant golden yellow, like the sun. Bright sunlight makes us feel positive and happy; if the sun burns too brightly, it is unbearable; and if sunlight is lacking we quickly feel depressed. This metaphor works well for the solar plexus chakra, which can be tricky to balance.

Main functions

This chakra has a strong link to the sense of self. Observe a small child having a tantrum – that is powerful solar plexus energy at work! The growing child must learn to master strong feelings of will in order to cooperate with others, using compassion and understanding. The balance between what the child wants and taking others into consideration is key to understanding this chakra.

Tiger's eye

Solar plexus chakra issues

The solar plexus chakra corresponds to the pancreas, the gland that produces insulin, which is the hormone that controls sugar levels in the body. Sugar – sweetness – is something we all desire; however, its effects fluctuate. On the physical level, an imbalance shows up as mood swings or

food cravings. Emotionally, strong feelings such as aggression or anger are key indicators of solar plexus disturbance. Taking slow and regular calm breaths can help restore the core energy of the body and rebalance this chakra. Eating slow-release carbohydrates such as oats can help regulate blood sugar levels.

How crystals can help

Tiger's eye has a powerful energising yet stabilising effect on the solar plexus chakra. Worn as a pendant or ring, or placed in the home or work environment, this crystal calms fluctuating solar plexus energies. Another crystal that works well here is citrine – yellow quartz – which has a cleansing effect that helps neutralise negative emotions.

Heart Chakra

The heart chakra is located in the centre of the chest, over the breastbone. Its name in Sanskrit is *anahata*, which means 'unbeaten'. Like the saying, 'Sticks and stones may break my bones, but words can never hurt me', a strong heart chakra is unaffected by emotional swings or harsh words, and answers negativity with love and compassion. Its primary colour is green, representing growth. It also has a secondary colour, pink, symbolising unconditional love.

Main functions

As well as corresponding to the organ of the heart and its associated emotion of love, the heart chakra also energises the thymus gland, which is located above the breastbone. The thymus gland helps maintain a healthy immune system – the body's defence against bacteria and viruses. The immune system is depleted by emotional stress or anxiety, so maintaining the energy of the heart chakra and keeping emotions positive helps maintain a healthy mind in a healthy body.

Aventurine

Heart chakra issues

Emotions such as sadness or feelings of rejection are typical signs of heart chakra depletion. The more separate we feel from others, the more the energy of the heart chakra is lowered. Like a plant deprived of water and food, we grow weak and lack vitality. Spending time in nature, breathing in fresh air and being in the sunlight help restore the energy of a depleted heart chakra, as does talking with understanding friends and helpers.

How crystals can help

Aventurine, with its rich green energy, is a wonderful support for the heart chakra, either worn as a pendant or carried as a power stone. It can also be placed in the bath to improve relaxation and sleep, which are both great restoratives when emotions are low. Pink rose quartz is another significant heart chakra stone, symbolic of unconditional love, gentleness and peace. Place a crystal under your pillow to help you sleep.

Throat Chakra

Vishuddha, the Sanskrit name for this chakra, means 'purification'. The throat chakra is the first of the higher chakras, which operate at a faster and more intense frequency than the lower energy centres. This delicately balanced area, located around the hollow at the base of the neck, is closely related to sound, communication and the voice. Its colour is vibrant blue. The throat chakra influences our interactions with the people around us, through the words we choose to say.

Sodalite

Main functions

Linked to the thyroid gland, the throat chakra is closely associated with metabolism, the way in which the body converts and uses energy. This chakra also is situated quite close to the thymus gland in the upper chest, which, as we have seen, plays an important role in the strength of our immune system and is linked to the heart chakra. Keeping positive emotions flowing through the heart centre is a good way to help support and strengthen the throat chakra. Within the chakra system, energy centres work together as well as individually.

Throat chakra issues

The throat chakra and its physical surroundings are prone to soreness and infection if the immune system is weak; these ailments are common signs of energy depletion. The throat area is also extremely sensitive to emotion – at times of stress, it may feel tight, constricted or painful, sometimes closing the throat chakra completely. At times like these, the heart centre below needs gentle healing with a crystal such as aventurine, to restore the flow of energy, and the throat needs treatment as described below.

How crystals can help

Sodalite is a cooling and soothing crystal to wear or place over the throat to calm emotional stress and help restore balance. Lapis lazuli, another vibrant blue stone, provides a revitalising and clarifying energy boost; it can be made into a crystal water or elixir and slowly sipped to help revive a depleted throat chakra.

Third Eye Chakra

The third eye chakra is so called because it is depicted on ancient Indian statues and manuscripts as being positioned between the eyebrows, in the centre of the forehead, in the shape of an eye. Its Sanskrit name is *ajna*, which means 'to perceive'. The third eye chakra is closely associated with perception beyond the ordinary bounds of the self and everyday life. This energy centre is connected with intuition, inspiration and leaps of consciousness. Its colour is a soothing deep purple or indigo.

Main functions

Physically, the third eye chakra is linked to the pituitary, a hormone-stimulating gland located behind the bridge of the nose at the base of the brain. The pituitary gland is responsible for regulating a variety of activities in the body linked to growth, reproductive function and sexual cycles, but in a sensitive and silent way that is far beyond the processes of the conscious or rational mind. Ancient practices such as yoga, an important part of Ayurveda, sought to balance human sexual energies with the higher frequencies of cosmic energy and the third eye was considered the portal that enabled this interaction to take place through meditation.

Amethyst

Third eye chakra issues

A depleted third eye chakra is revealed through frontal headaches or eyestrain, with pain across the front of the forehead. This pain is a sign that the intuitive mind is not being allowed to express itself. Too often, creativity is crushed under the weight of rational thinking; however, leaps of consciousness from the third eye can provide new, unusual solutions to challenges.

How crystals can help

Amethyst is the classic Master Healing Crystal for the third eye, and stones that are deep purple in colour are especially effective. When placed on the forehead, amethyst soothes and calms the extremely sensitive third eye chakra and opens it to new levels of perception. Another useful crystal is sugilite, which has a clarifying effect that increases levels of perception and understanding.

Crown Chakra

The crown chakra sits at the middle of the top of the head, where the bones of the skull are still open in a newborn baby. Ancient Indian tradition maintains that this opening allows the soul to enter the body at birth. The name of the crown chakra in Sanskrit is *sahasrara*, or 'thousand-petaled lotus'. During a person's lifetime, this centre connects to the soul and the source of its eternal wisdom. Its colour is white, a diamond brilliance filled with rainbow reflections.

Main functions

The crown chakra corresponds to the pineal gland, located deep within the skull and responsible for the secretion of melatonin, a hormone that controls the body's biological clock. This hormone influences periods of wakefulness and sleep, or states of consciousness and unconsciousness. Dreams can be interpreted as information from the crown chakra, and many indigenous cultures regard dreams as direct communication from the level of the soul.

Crown chakra issues

Lack of full-spectrum daylight can disrupt the pineal gland, causing the depression and disrupted sleep patterns known as Seasonal Affective Disorder (SAD). SAD is one of the most common signs of crown chakra imbalance. The crown chakra is also extremely sensitive to stress of any kind – physical, emotional, mental or environmental – which can result in mood swings, an erratic temper or confusion. A state of extreme mental unrest is also a sign of a depleted crown chakra in need of healing.

How crystals can help

Clear quartz

Clear quartz is the Master Healing Crystal that corresponds to the crown chakra and has a sparkling and purifying effect. Placing clear quartz over the crown of the head gives the body an energy shower that cleans away negativity and toxicity. Another helpful crystal is clear danburite, which has a gentler, more soothing, cleansing effect. Placing red jasper between the feet is important to balance both these stones and to keep the body grounded.

Alternative Chakra Healing Crystals

The following six pages show some alternative healing crystals which you may like to collect to help balance and restore the different chakra energies.

Stones for the root chakra

Ruby: A deep-red precious stone, also available in rough pieces that are less expensive than finished gems. Ruby provides strength to the blood and circulation and increases physical vitality.

Smoky quartz: Its brown colour connects it to the Earth. Smoky quartz is a powerful cleanser and detoxifier as well as a good grounding crystal.

Stones for the sacral chakra

AMBER: A warm, orange-yellow organic mineral, which is the fossilised resin of prehistoric pine trees. Amber promotes positive feelings and cheerfulness, as well as openness to others.

ORANGE CALCITE: A soft apricot-orange crystal, easy to obtain. Orange calcite has a gentle effect on the sacral chakra and works well with children to ease upset feelings and restore calm.

Stones for the solar plexus chakra

GOLDEN TOPAZ: A bright, golden-yellow precious stone. Topaz is a powerful amplifier of solar plexus energy.

CITRINE: Golden quartz, which supports physical energy and vitality and attracts abundance.

Alternative Chakra Healing Crystals

Stones for the heart chakra

Rose quartz: A pale pink quartz. Rose quartz is the classic crystal to promote feelings of love, peace and healing. It is a popular crystal with both adults and children, especially when worn over the heart chakra.

Green fluorite: A rare, vibrant green fluorite with a geometric structure, good for creating a stable and balanced feeling in the heart.

Amazonite: A speckled, slightly blue-green stone, good for enabling loving communication and promoting a good balance between the heart and throat chakras.

Stones for the throat chakra

BLUE LACE AGATE: A pale-blue microcrystalline quartz with white flecks. Blue lace agate is a gentle and calming crystal which has a soothing effect on the throat chakra.

LAPIS LAZULI: A deep royal-blue stone, sacred to the Egyptian Pharaohs. Lapis lazuli promotes communication at the highest and most spiritual levels.

SAPPHIRE: A precious dark-blue gemstone, very expensive, but a brilliant tonic to the throat chakra, stimulating clear and powerful personal expression.

Stones for the third eye chakra

SUGILITE: An opaque stone with a speckled purple appearance, excellent for amplifying spiritual awareness. Sugilite also brings meaningful dreams.

CHAROITE: An unusual stone with purple, white, grey and black flecks and a shimmering appearance. Charoite amplifies spiritual energy and increases psychic awareness.

LAVENDER QUARTZ: An unusual pale lilac-coloured crystal, with a gentle and calming effect on mental stress. Lavender quartz eases feelings of overload and promotes restful sleep.

Stones for the crown chakra

DANBURITE: A clear crystal with a wedge-like inner structure. Danburite is gentler in effect than quartz and facilitates connections to angelic guides and high levels of spiritual wisdom.

HERKIMER DIAMOND: A special type of quartz with a small and precisely defined geometric shape. Herkimer diamond sharpens and clarifies spiritual perception.

SELENITE: A cloudy white mineral that forms in flat blades, selenite has a calming and soothing effect on the crown chakra, easing mental stress and harmonising the emotions.

Crystals for Wellbeing

CRYSTALS FOR PHYSICAL ISSUES

BACK ACHE (TO EASE)	Carnelian, red jasper, amber
BLOOD CIRCULATION (TO IMPROVE)	Red jasper, ruby, bloodstone
BONES (TO STRENGTHEN)	Green or purple fluorite
CHRONIC FATIGUE SYNDROME	Ruby, amber, amethyst
DETOXIFICATION (TO EASE)	Smoky quartz, clear quartz, Herkimer diamond
FERTILITY (TO IMPROVE)	Rose quartz, ruby, carnelian
HEADACHES (TO EASE)	Rose quartz, amethyst, lavender quartz
HIGH BLOOD PRESSURE (TO REDUCE)	Rose quartz, amethyst, sodalite
HORMONE IMBALANCE	Amber, carnelian, blue moonstone
IMMUNE SUPPORT	Clear quartz, aventurine, citrine
MENOPAUSE SUPPORT	Rose quartz, carnelian, amethyst
MENSTRUAL SUPPORT	Carnelian, amber, white moonstone

WARNING

Remember: crystals and their healing properties are not a replacement for proper medical advice.

CRYSTALS FOR MOODS AND EMOTIONS

ANGER (TO CALM)	Rose quartz, carnelian, sodalite
ANXIETY (TO EASE)	Rose quartz, amethyst, aventurine
BURNOUT (TO EASE)	Ruby, carnelian, tiger's eye
CONFIDENCE (TO IMPROVE)	Amber, orange calcite, carnelian
CREATIVITY (TO STIMULATE)	Amethyst, clear quartz, danburite
DEPRESSION (TO EASE)	Amethyst, blue lace agate, rose quartz
EMOTIONAL STRESS (TO EASE)	Amethyst, lavender quartz, aventurine
FEAR (TO SOOTHE)	Amethyst, sodalite, carnelian
GRIEF (TO EASE)	Rose quartz, amethyst, sugilite
IMPOTENCE/INTIMACY ISSUES (TO REDUCE)	Rose quartz, ruby, carnelian
INSOMNIA FROM STRESS (TO REDUCE)	Aventurine, amazonite, peridot
JOY (TO INCREASE)	Citrine, tiger's eye, carnelian
LOVE (TO ATTRACT)	Rose quartz, lavender quartz, ruby
MEDITATION (TO IMRPOVE FOCUS)	Clear quartz, amethyst, sodalite
PEACE (TO BRING INTO ONE'S LIFE)	Lavender quartz, amethyst, blue moonstone
SHYNESS (TO DECREASE)	Carnelian, amber, citrine

Birthstone and Zodiac Charts

These charts associate different crystals with the months of the year (called birthstones) or with zodiac signs. These charts can be useful if you are choosing crystals for a friend, to correspond with either the birth month or the astrological sign.

BIRTHSTONES

JANUARY	Garnet, rose quartz	JULY	Ruby, carnelian
FEBRUARY	Amethyst, onyx	AUGUST	Peridot, sardonyx
MARCH	Aquamarine, bloodstone	SEPTEMBER	Sapphire, lapis lazuli
APRIL	Diamond, clear quartz	OCTOBER	Opal, tourmaline
MAY	Emerald, chrysoprase	NOVEMBER	Topaz, citrine
JUNE	Pearl, moonstone	DECEMBER	Tanzanite, turquoise

This list is often used by jewellers

ZODIAC CRYSTALS

ARIES (21 Mar–19 Apr)	Carnelian, jasper, ruby, diamond, kunzite, bloodstone
TAURUS (20 Apr–20 May)	Aquamarine, tourmaline, topaz, emerald, tiger's eye
GEMINI (21 May–20 Jun)	Citrine, tiger's eye, chrysocolla, pearl, apophyllite
CANCER (21 Jun–22 Jul)	Pearl, moonstone, emerald, ruby, amber
LEO (23 Jul–22 Aug)	Sunstone, clear quartz, ruby, turquoise, spinel
VIRGO (23 Aug–22 Sep)	Carnelian, citrine, sapphire, peridot, sugilite
LIBRA (23 Sep–22 Oct)	Opal, lapis lazuli, peridot, aventurine, jade
SCORPIO (23 Oct–21 Nov)	Kunzite, Herkimer diamond, aquamarine, malachite, dioptase
SAGITTARIUS (22 Nov–21 Dec)	Smoky quartz, turquoise, malachite, spinel, blue lace agate
CAPRICORN (22 Dec–19 Jan)	Onyx, jet, ruby, garnet, labradorite
AQUARIUS (20 Jan–18 Feb)	Amethyst, aquamarine, angelite, blue chalcedony, sapphire
PISCES (19 Feb–20 Mar)	Calcite, turquoise, pearl, fluorite

Birthstone and Zodiac Charts

Resources

Contact these organisations if you are interested in training as a crystal healer or if you are seeking a qualified therapist in your area.

UK CRYSTAL HEALING ASSOCIATIONS

ACHO [Affiliation of Crystal Healing Organisations]
PO BOX 100
Exminster
Exeter
Devon EX6 8YT
Tel. 07837 696 301
www.crystal-healing.org

IACHT [International Association of Crystal Healing Therapists]
PO BOX 344
Manchester M60 2EZ
Tel 01200 426061
www.iacht.co.uk

Crystal Healing Federation
Tel 0870 760 7195
www.crystalandhealing.com

USA CRYSTAL HEALING ASSOCIATIONS

Association of Melody Crystal Healing Instructors
www.taomchi.com

The Crystal Academy of Advanced Healing Arts
www.webcrytstalacademy.com

AUSTRALIAN CRYSTAL HEALING ASSOCIATIONS

NATURAL THERAPY
PAGES RESOURCE DIRECTORY
www.naturaltherapypages.com.
au/therapy/Crystal_Therapy

THE KARYNA CENTRE
PO BOX 117
Rozelle 2039
NSW Australia
www.crystalsoundandlight.com

CRYSTAL SUPPLIERS [UK]

CRYSTAL PLANET [RICHARD SCULL]
www.crystal-planet.com
SARA GILLARD
www.crystalvine.co.uk
MIKE JACKSON
www.thecrystalman.co.uk

BIOGRAPHY

JENNIE HARDING, BA, TIDHA, MIPTI, HNC,
has 20 years' experience as a healer working with
various approaches, including crystals, essential
oils, herbs, crystal energy remedies, incense,
and natural beauty techniques. She is the author
of 16 books. From 1992–2005 she was senior
Essential Oil Therapeutics tutor at the Tisserand
Aromatherapy Institute.

Index

PICTURE CREDITS

The publishers would like to thank the following for permission to use images. **Getty**/Kelvin Murray: 11, 45. **iStockphoto**/Matthew Bowden: 32; Graeme Purdy: 36; Katherine Newman: 46; Matej Pribelsky: 54; Lucwa: 59; Andreas Karelias: 65; Saluha: 66. **Corbis**/Image 100: 34; Mina Chapman: 40; Chris Rogers: 48; Steve and Ann Toon/Robert Harding World Imagery: 57. **Alamy**/Jon Arnold: 61.